Why can't we stop!

Why can't we stop!

How to avoid menticide: the 2020's cause of
acting & thinking recklessly

Tom Pickering

Winningthinking.uk®

"The privilege of a lifetime is to become who you truly are." Carl Jung

How to avoid menticide: the 2020's cause of acting & thinking recklessly

This is the know-how to free yourself, become aware of, and have the skills to avoid menticide. Menticide is the 2020's systemic Tech and the cultural threat that is destroying your humanity and your mind.

It took a few strong people to unravel the terror of the Gulags in Russia, not the masses. That might be you?

Whilst technology is accelerating this demise, menticide is nothing new. For example, in the UK during the 1500s, **menticide** justified burning at the stake as a form of execution for women found guilty of witchcraft. Most accusations of witchcraft did not originate in the church but resulted from local personal rivalries and disputes.

Why Can't We Stop?

We're under threat. A threat that, left unnoticed, will culminate in mass hysteria.

It's time to bridge the gap and question this threat of menticide because if left to seep into our subconscious and we don't understand how to tackle it, our voices will diminish. One by one.

From the Bible and best practice to hundreds of company turnarounds, psychological analysis and a summary of the strategic shifts of the 2020-2021 crisis, the author draws on an eclectic range of sources to summarise his message for further consideration.

The intention of this book is not to brainwash you into the author's way of thinking. Rather, the purpose of this pragmatic and practical book is to highlight the dire crisis society faces, encourage intelligent debate and provide you, the reader, with the knowledge to take back control.

So what are we facing? Are people simply becoming increasingly stupid? Or is tech getting cleverer? Are the boundaries between logic and illogic becoming so blurred we can't think straight? How do can we handle the tyrannical views and shallow ideologies that swamp the media? Are we looking high enough up for our answers?

Let's start the debate.

More recently very few saw the rise of the Nazi party either and when they did, no one listened and it was too late.

(Unknown Source thought to be taken in a 1930s German shipyard.)

This book is written in the context of these 3 books in the series for executive leaders:

ISBN	Title
978-1-9196337-0-1	The Evil in Silence - hardback
978-1-9196337-1-8	The Evil in Silence - ebook
978-1-9196337-2-5	You Have Infinite Ability - hardback
978-1-9196337-3-2	You Have Infinite Ability - ebook
978-1-9196337-4-9	The Psychology and Pathology of Big Tech - hardback
978-1-9196337-5-6	The Psychology and Pathology of Big Tech - ebook
978-1-9196337-6-3	Why can't you stop? menticide ebook
978-1-9196337-7-0	Why can't you stop? hardback

"He who dictates and formulates the words and phrases we use, he who is master of the press and radio, is master of the mind." —— Joost A.M. Meerloo, *The Rape of the Mind: The Psychology of Thought Control, Menticide, and Brainwashing*

It feels weird to watch a car crash in slow motion that so few can see or say anything about?

The importance of this philosophical question is becoming critical to our human and business survival on every front, environment, sustainability, wellbeing, profits, relationships, peace, dialogue, etc:

1. "Do we have the courage to recognise a God?"
2. "Do we think we can set our own purpose and values i.e. know better?"
3. "What do we love and or who / what do we worship?"

Aetheastism seems to be creating an endless list of tyrannical low-level shallow ideologies, with endless unintended consequences. Technology is recklessly accelerating and fuelling the process of inflaming dialogue. Online communication does not accommodate different views.

So are we looking high enough?

This book explores some of the consequences and opens up this debate and solutions.

The good news is that this threat and the unique set of winningthinking® skills my team has created enables us to be uniquely and peculiarly familiar with the challenge and there is a simple solution to it. That said, I am primarily a strategist, an executive operator, and doer.

But, you do face an unprecedented threat engulfing society that few recognise, understand, and at worse can't escape – menticide, broadly the destroying of your mind.

"Where thinking is isolated without free exchange with other minds and can no longer expand, delusion may follow. Whenever ideas are compartmentalized, behind and between curtains, the process of continual alert confrontation of facts and reality is hampered. The system freezes, becomes rigid, and dies of delusion."—— Joost A.M. Meerloo

I observe, and I am concerned you are facing a threat you don't see, and increasingly unless you act against the threat, your ability to influence, maintain your awareness, and capability to cope with the scenario, now and in the future, will exponentially diminish and the risks will exponentially escalate too!

This is a pragmatic summary checked from the broadest perspectives, drawn from hundreds of company turnarounds, observations on best practices, detailed psychological analysis, and strategic shifts drawn from the 2020-2021 period.

At its simplest level, I explore why we live in an environment that no longer meets our human needs and is one we can't make sense of.

The good news is that the solution can be achieved in a day, is remarkably simple, yet difficult. But most leaders don't see the need or connection.

The key capability in organizations is to:

1. Create a great place to work that: values individuals and lets them do their jobs in their own way
2. Seamlessly adjust to the target and strategy as it shifts
3. Take new action, and understand what is preventing new action
4. Work in a way that builds capabilities, relationships, and profits on the job

As the specialist winningthinking/icebreaker team, we capture this using the jazz band metaphor https://www.winningthinking.uk/jazz-band/

However, there are forces at play subconsciously usurping your agenda, the mechanism which needs to be understood to recognise their traits and mechanisms.

1. *The Evil of Silence: Woke Culture And The Mechanics Of Tyranny*
2. *The Psychology & Pathology of BigTech: Technology is now the dominant parasite and the psychological pathology that has reduced you & your business to dope on a rope*

3. *The 2020s The Decade of Menticide? Your Choice. What is the link between burning witches at the stake, BigTech, and how to avoid the destroying of your humanity and mind?*

My motivation is captured in my last book that "You have infinite capability: and you can regain what good looks like. But until you understand the three, 1-3 above, intertwined forces trying to get control of yourself and your business and dupe you off your agenda, you have no chance of getting ahead."

The exciting part of this is that the One-day team winningthinking.uk game-changer strategy workshops we run on the Ashridge Business School Campus can resolve all of these issues in one day.

Whilst you really need to walk through the process with your team together in the context of your business objectives, I hope these books provide new perspectives that trigger some fresh thinking to enable you to transform your business.

The question is do you realise what is driving you and stopping you from achieving your desired personal and business outcomes for you and your peers?

If you have any questions or observations feel free to reach out on email tom@winningthinking.uk.

PS. This book gets back to basics, so is even checked from a pragmatic biblical perspective, because it's quite clear that even people's own ideology is insufficient and is causing substantial unintended consequences at scale, so ideology and low-level fixes are not fixing the issues.

Enjoy.

Tom Pickering CEO

icebreakerexecutive.com™ and winningthinking.uk®

©Tom Pickering 2021

Contents

Why do we live in a culture that doesn't now meet our needs?

Are people getting increasingly stupid, whilst tech is getting cleverer?

Do we want these tech outcomes? Why do we think these tech outcomes are inevitable?

A divided vision of the future:
Leaders are torn about what the shift means for them

The leaders we surveyed agree, we're on the verge of immense change. More than eight in ten (82 percent) leaders expect humans and machines will work as integrated teams within their organization inside of five years (26 percent say their workforce and machines are already successfully working this way). However, they're divided by what this shift will mean for them, their business and even the world at large.

We can see this divide in the way that leaders forecast the future. Fifty percent of business leaders think automated systems will free-up their time - meaning one in two don't share this view. More than four in ten (42 percent) believe they'll have more job satisfaction in the future by offloading the tasks they don't want to do to machines - suggesting 58 percent believe something to the contrary, and stand to miss out on the opportunity to harness automated systems to free-up their time for higher order pursuits with a focus on creativity, education and strategy. Almost six in ten (56 percent) say schools will need to teach how to learn rather than what to learn to prepare students for jobs that don't exist yet (corroborating IFTF's forecast that 85 percent of jobs that will exist in 2030 haven't been invented yet) - but 44 percent disagree. These differing viewpoints could make it difficult for business leaders to confidently prepare for a future that's in flux.

> " *More than eight in ten (82 percent) leaders expect humans and machines will work as integrated teams within their organization inside of five years.* "

Dell Technologies | 3

Source Dell: Realizing-2030-A-Divided-Vision-of-the-Future-Summary.pdf

What is the source of wisdom in your organisation?
Why should we completely revisit what is right or wrong in business?

The infinite element is through a connection with God or else your limit is you!

A real crisis such as Covid 19 sorts out what and who is important and it's crucial not to ignore and apply the learning. Ignoring this leaves an internal misalignment which can be like an itch you won't scratch and becomes very stressful.

It seems very clear that with the level of dysfunctionality, anger, and unintended societal, environmental consequences taking place right now, we have been found out. So we are unable to set our own ethics, purpose, and values in business.

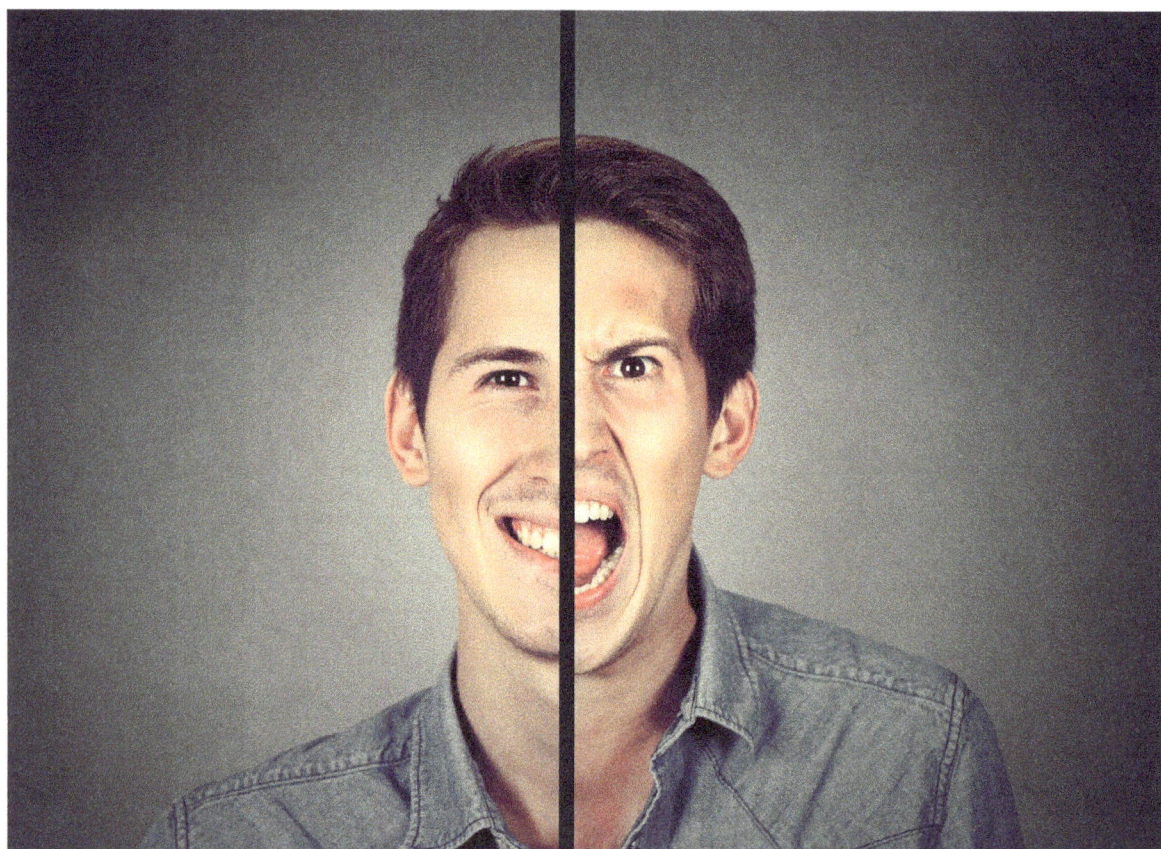

Do you think you have sufficient wisdom to navigate your current scenario, and know where to turn to when you struggle?

Society and businesses are facing an epidemic of smearing individuals without debate. Debate is tough and the sign of wisdom requires people to understand that wisdom comes from something higher. Considering that we might be that source of wisdom is an interesting territory, which works until you face a tough challenge. Is it easier to avoid debate than resolve tough issues?

Even good secular attempts, driven by the smartest people, to resolve issues such as the Project Oxygen at Google are reported to have unwound. Even the best secular efforts to close the leadership gap without having a satisfactory source of wisdom, creates an endless stream of unintended consequences and misalignment:

- 10% of the directors promoted to a vice-president level position were recipients of Google's Great Manager Award.
- It is not enough to highlight the high scores, especially in a working environment that produces game-changing applications like Google .(Savic & Shi, 2010).

So secular institutions have no implicit wisdom.

Our intelligence is determined by our ability to fix problems which are largely determined by our relationships with those around us., and whether we fix the right problems depends upon whether our thinking is being challenged or checking if our "truths" are true.

So, if technology erodes these bonds between us and our relationships and quality of dialogue, are we are starting to behave stupidly like machines? Is this machine-like behaviour evidenced by our increasingly binary or polarised views and the inability to debate, so we start behaving like "non-thinking," just "doing" machines?

If this is the case in an increasingly technological society, the machines sure will win.

People do want to put humanity at the centre of a business, but do we understand what it is to be human?

So how do we regain morality?

It wasn't the majority that unwound and exposed the Gulags, it was a few incredibly strong individuals. So we must re-engage the minority that cares, and let them take a lead again and listen to those that we don't agree with?

But from where do we derive our wisdom to stand up against what we believe is wrong?

Mass hysteria or mass psychosis

Mass hysteria or mass psychosis is an extreme form of groupthink when members of the group follow the consensus instead of thinking critically and valuing the truth and healthy open debate to inform decisions.

George Orwell said, "in a time of universal deceit, telling the truth is a revolutionary act!"

"What is needed now is a swift cold shower of reality. The time for self-harming distractions with "wokus pocus," obsessing about sexual dysmorphia, Marxist "critical race theory" and "climate catastrophism" ... - all of which the Chinese Communist Party is glad to encourage - must end." GateStone Institute 19/8/21

Consider this: What are you too afraid to discuss that you know needs challenging and thinking through?

Purposelessness

Over the last 40 years since the 1970s, there has been a switch away from frugality and common sense to "more." This has evolved into the mantras of growth and domination and the hyper valuation of tech companies.

These mantras have been found out during the Covid-19 pandemic with a shift and realisation of the importance of relationships and profit. The crisis has shone a light on who the heroes actually are: that is the nurses and not leaders or social media influencers.

Yet the growth and domination mantras continue to be fuelled by a tech engulfed consumption growth-driven society, and social media, and a loss of purpose.

"Man cannot stand a meaningless life. The least of things with a meaning is worth more in life than the greatest of things without it." Carl Jung

"The only meaningful life is a life that strives for the individual realization — absolute and unconditional — of its own particular law. To the extent that a man is untrue to the law of his being, he has failed to realize his own life's meaning." Carl Jung

So, a significant wellbeing gap in businesses has opened, highlighting increasingly the meaningless purpose of many businesses, as well as a non-compelling proposition, particularly businesses centred around tech.

How we have lost control of technology is raised in The Pathology and Psychology of Big Tech. Leaders / big4 are pushing more tech and driving the propaganda to influence the mass thinking to a tech end as if tech is inevitable.

So, do we need to start doing meaningful things and realign our businesses accordingly?

These are the top 7 strategic learnings we have drawn from the 2020–2021 period.

Our future depends upon building a better world:

The 7 permanent shifts for CEOs to action to avoid the race – bottom:

1. Create Work for all levels: protect Employment
2. Increase Prices and Profit: reduce consumption
3. Re-Use: reduce consumption, protect the planet
4. People Relationships: reduce suicide *1 etc.
5. Reduce Online / Tech; less addiction regain self *1
6. Support Local and Community: enable mutual success
7. Intimacy: Acknowledge and Value Everyone's View

Underlying focus for success – "Put Others First"

icebreaker
winning thinking

5

Getting in control of technology

Whilst the issue with technology is a psychological one, causing this mass psychosis, the notion that technology will self-correct, and laws realign to meet our needs, is probably flawed.

Why? Because technology is unlike humans. Tech is tireless, moves too fast, does not follow our logic, and impact at a time when, until now, we have never really needed to understand humanity, let alone the psychological impact of this deluge of technology on the basics of humanity and life.

Whilst Hitler or any other tyrant eventually got found out and shamed or usurped by the masses propagating their demise, a demise of technology is unlikely because in a tech-fuelled society our ability to organise ourselves and have meaningful debate across divides is rapidly diminishing. Conflict is increasing. Free speech is the means to correct and make sense of the challenge, not tech!

I think it follows that the emergence of binary thinking and polarisation and echo chambers are akin to people beginning to imitate technology, thereby becoming more like machines, and we are becoming far less interested in others' views or valuing people for who they are.

What are the underlying interests and drivers of technology?

Economic rent; stripped $100bn from the economy

Thirty years ago, economist William Baumol worried about the rise of "unproductive entrepreneurs" who buy up rivals or use regulations to stifle competition, **thriving as parasites on productive parts of the economy.**

Economic rent

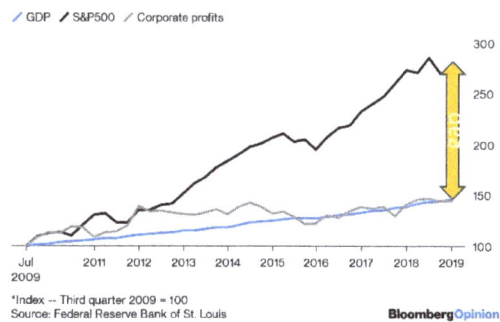

GDP S&P500 Corporate profits

*Index -- Third quarter 2009 = 100
Source: Federal Reserve Bank of St. Louis

BloombergOpinion

Ethics and avoiding getting drawn into menticide

I think it's accurate to say current tech, purpose, values, and cultural strategies are encouraging mass psychosis, which is the bedrock of menticide.

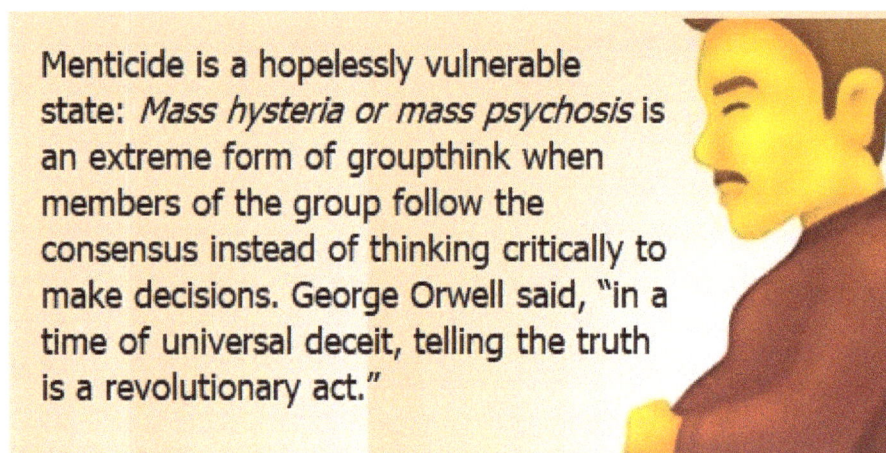

Menticide is a hopelessly vulnerable state: *Mass hysteria or mass psychosis* is an extreme form of groupthink when members of the group follow the consensus instead of thinking critically to make decisions. George Orwell said, "in a time of universal deceit, telling the truth is a revolutionary act."

Unicom's pregnant man emoji

Mass psychogenic or mass hysteria is the rapid spread of illness affecting members of a cohesive group.

Mass hysteria was the cause of burning witches in the Middle Ages. The tools like cancel culture are akin to victimhood, scapegoating, and punishment that underly technology-centric solutions tools. Technology by its nature is binary, so doesn't accommodate free speech or free-thinking.

The process of menticide is common to tech or other tyrannies:

"There is another important weapon the totalitarians use in their campaign to frighten the world into submission. This is the weapon of psychological shock. Hitler kept his enemies in a state of constant confusion and diplomatic upheaval. They never knew what this unpredictable madman was going to do next. Hitler was never logical because he knew that that was what he was expected to be. Logic can be met with logic, while illogic cannot—it confuses those who think straight. The Big Lie and monotonously repeated nonsense have more emotional appeal in a cold war than logic and reason. While the enemy is still searching for a reasonable counter-argument to the first lie, the totalitarians can assault him with another."

—— Joost A.M. Meerloo, *The Rape of the Mind: The Psychology of Thought Control, Menticide, and Brainwashing*

What does good look like?

"The privilege of a lifetime is to become who you truly are." Carl Jung

I would add "and be valued for and surrounded by people who are interested in who you are."
A crisis sorts out what is important and who is important.

Consider this hypothesis:
We are ALL flawed and highly reliant on each other, and we can afford to isolate our "enemies."
From a Christian perspective, Jesus presented the toughest challenge for us, we should "Love our enemies".

From my experience, the number of CEOs and boards who are asking "how do we gain trust, how do we do the right thing by our employees, right things by our customers, and the right things by the shareholders" has only increased.

Tim Ryan CEO PWC

It is the wrong people who are suffering
People who care and are losing the courage to speak out, and when they do speak against the common wisdom they get attacked and unfairly labelled. This is leading to a moral decline because those that don't care, prefer to smear, destroy, and come to the fore, while the wrong types begin to thrive. This requires new skills to cope with and navigate too, captured in our book *The Evil of Silence.*

Purposeless

Getting in control of technology

Whilst the issue with technology is a psychological one, causing this mass psychosis, the notion that technology will self-correct and laws realign to meet our needs, is flawed because technology is unlike humans, is tireless, moves too fast, is irrational, and impacting at a time when we have never really needed to understand humanity, let alone the psychological impact of technology on humanity.

And or unlike Hitler or any other tyrant, they eventually got found out and usurped by the masses propagating their demise.

In the case of technology, a demise of technology is unlikely because in a tech-fuelled society our ability to organise ourselves and have meaningful debate across divides is rapidly diminishing, conflict is increasing and so is free speech.

Such binary thinking, polarisation and echo chambers are akin to people imitating technology and becoming more like machines?

The "good" versus "evil" narrative

So, the challenge is raised in terms of what is the source of morality and what is right or wrong. This must go beyond making money on the crazed valuations of bitcoin, and secular leadership strategies.

This parasitic type of tech investment is taking cash, investment, and resources from and weakening the productive economy and defi/crypto for example reducing solvency of the banks that caused the 2008 banking crash too.

The hierarchy of business ethics is driven by

- Truth
- The society impact
- Faith/ethics

The attempts to define a personal secular sense of "good" morality leads to idolatry and conflict, and those that fall outside these ideals are "evil." This is a dangerous, highly sensitive territory because ethics based upon faith or any other woke criteria are subjective and difficult to rationalise.

In 2012, likes and shares changed everything on social media, and its social impact has become far more harmful.

So social media fuels this activism, echo chambers, and moralism, leading to blind blindness where truth is not valued nor is it emotive, motivating, or appealing.

"There is no coming to consciousness without pain." Carl Jung

The pain and or difficulty in doing the RIGHT thing, can be confused with doing the wrong thing so fall foul of and be confused with the woke notion of taking offence, so one can be falsely accused of denying the "lived experience" unable to action a sensible solution!

This raises the question what are we as human beings?

We are love machines, machines; the tricky thing is this:

"what do we love?"

At the very top level, we have a choice to follow the first commandment "to love God and other people". Jesus said there is no greater law than this.

There are dramatic implications and challenges that Jesus went on to identify:

- Love thy enemies
- Forgive and show grace

The most realistic place for us to experience "imposter syndrome" or feel constantly humbled. What good looks like paradoxically is to realise that we are all flawed and we do not know better.

The most realistic, safest place for us is imposter syndrome or constantly humbled or to realise that we are all flawed and do not know better. Humility is the most natural place to be because we know so little of what there is to know, and far more that we don't know. Open your eyes and see the beauty, look outside the window and its impossibility around the detail: why or how do leaves decompose?

Socrates evidenced that our survival and success are entirely dependent upon others. Others to challenge our thinking, and or wellbeing based upon our willingness to listen, take an interest in different views and support each other.

Grace and love are critical to avoid conflict and the means to quell anger.

So, who do we turn to, a tolerant model or a secular idolatry-driven model that leads to idolatry?

Idolatry happens if we look too low and or ignore the fact there is an infinite source of higher wisdom or a God. Conscience or wisdom is clearly external and ethics a heart-driven thing that doesn't, as Google noted with their Oxygen Program, fit neatly with typical metrics.

We tend to create idolatry even though it may sound great, therefore it is incomplete so has unintended consequences. The negative unintended consequences, which we can see are all around us affecting:

- Mental health
- Social media and driven conflict
- Sustainability and consumption
- Tech-driven satisfaction like / share usurping our natural face-to-face systems
- Free speech
- Fractious relationships
- Profit
- Tyranny control
- Critical thinking and healthy open debate and the value of truth
- Woke mantras victimhood etc

Social systems are checked by teams, whereas tech is vulnerable to waves of disinformation below:

So, who can or should set morals – God or us? If we think we know better and set them, history suggests this tends to lead to war, and utopia tends to destroy foes.

ED 🖼 Enrique **Dans**   IINNOVATION   FUTURE   SPAIN | MY BOOKS

CORPORATE
CULTURE
@ GOOGLE

Suddenly, at Google it's get on the program or get out

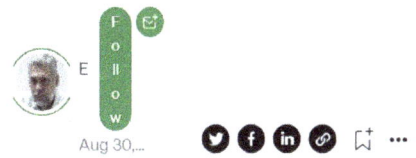

E   Follow

Aug 30,...

The party's over, everyone back to work. Someone has run out of patience at Google and a a corporate culture marked by freedom of expression, open debate and conversations on all issues in any field has been consigned to the past.

medium.com/enrique-dans/suddenly-at-google-its-get-on-the-program-or-get-out-5ce19930f554

What can we rally around?

We seem to have a God-shaped hole and if we were made to be addicted, were we made to be addicted to Jesus, not or digitalisation/social media. Addiction to social goes some way to explain why we may becoming and or become more akin to technology than people?

Dr. Maté believes that addiction (or what we love) is not a choice, neither is it all about drugs and illicit substances, addiction affects most of us – whether it be to alcohol, nicotine, sugar, work, or exercise...the list is endless. He calls for a compassionate approach toward addiction, whether in ourselves or others. As he puts it, the question we need to ask is not why the addiction, but why the pain.

Why do we now live in a culture that doesn't meet our human needs?

It seems that technology is an addiction:

"addiction is manifested in temp pleasure that therefore we crave with negative outcomes in the long term and inability to give it up." Dr. Gabor Mate

Yet, if the outcome of loving God is good for us and we are addicted that's surely a good thing?

And if the idolatry or mantras are ones of intolerance, that's sure limiting personal development, truth, beauty, and or fuelling conflict?

Liberal democracy is a tyranny of tolerance. Because forcing people to be tolerant actually is forcing people to stay silent and go along with subjects that have a multitude of different views: such as abortion, gay marriage, or the multitude of identity politics-related perspectives.

If we can rally around one tolerant God that is alive, knows better, and had sorted this, life would surely still be challenging but far easier? So, if we loved that God and other people, we probably wouldn't go too far wrong!

Rational factual approaches to trying to define secular society moral codes are just boring.

So it seems that our God, such as Jesus, must be **someone or a person** so that we can emulate and imitate in order to be interesting or engaging?

Inanimate truths are of less or no interest, unengaging, meaningless, and just boring or in the case of China boring and tyrannical?

President Xi forces this ideal on Chinese Christians and Uyghurs by forcing them to memorise his speeches, almost putting Xi himself in the position of a God-like role model!

Role models

We need to have something to worship, and it seems that it must be a person or human role model in order to engage us.

Technology, however, seeks to control our attention and so manipulate us with devastating implications on our wellbeing and personal journey of self-discovery.

It's not easy either, and or we need a mentor which in the Christian tradition is Jesus. We look for role models in life although Christians are flawed role models because they naturally fall far short of Jesus who was God.

"The sad truth is that man's real-life consists of a complex of inexorable opposites — day and night, birth and death, happiness and misery, good and evil. We are not even sure that one will prevail against the other, that good will overcome evil, or joy defeat pain. Life is a battleground. It always has been and always will be; and if it were not so, existence would come to an end." Carl Jung

Feedback loops and the threat to liberal democracy

Bad ideas dominate engagement on social media because we don't react or respond to positive news, so bad ideas tend to dominate online ethics and these tech online echo chambers.

This (negative) feedback loop leads to depression, no thinking, and "just doing." Doing is sub-conscious-driven activity, that involves **no thinking** so we lose sight of a common good.

Gen Z has been impacted most by the "like and share upgrade" to social media which has been so harmful and caused their mental health to suffer the worst. Their thinking is dominated by trivia rather than learning about anything useful beyond their direct social influence, so they are trapped.

This trap of negative-positive feedback, conflict, the dominance of negativity, reduced thinking, the threat of being labelled as the evil one, and the trap is a threat to social democracy.

Yet materially, things are getting better since the 1970s. In the 1970s there were sensible material reasons for crises such as the 1973 Oil Crisis. Now the reasons for the crisis are less obvious, and we are losing sight of why we are unsatisfied or what "good looks like."

It begs the question of whether the post-2012 generation will ever experience what "good" looks like, and if so, how might they experience this?

Truth

Valuing truth should be the tool to irradicate falsehoods, but people find meaning and purpose in these falsehoods like postmodernism; the BLM movement; identity politics; and wokeness or victim culture that tries to conveniently destroy truth on the basis that science is just another of man's fiction.

These are general (and exclusive so divisor) mantras such as "Black Lives Matter" and or "stable coins." Generalisations are attractive and create an almost God-like position because they create certainty, fervour, and purpose fuelling dismantling of faith-centric certainty and the attractiveness and growth in tech-enabling echo chambers and of a self-righteous high ground during the pandemic. Yet God is the probably only constant to provide certainty.

People cannot operate without certainty. Indeed people will knowingly take the wrong action to reach certainty because they know it is wrong and unchallenged. Although when challenged, as the action is wrong, it's undefendable, and they smear critics and get angry to defend their purpose, position, and passion.

FAMGA stocks outperform since the pandemic

% change in stock price vs. % change in S&P 500 (3/11/20 – 9/1/20)

- Apple
- Amazon
- Facebook
- Microsoft
- Google
- S&P 500

Source: cbinsights.com, FactSet

CBINSIGHTS

Reaching the truth has become filled with fear in this terrifying social media environment because people who challenge China Wuhan lab as to the source of the virus, have been accused of being racist. Racism is a vicious accusation, and of course flawed, and the Wuhan source is a sensible challenge?

Wikipedia has shown how to create the best online content: created from different viewpoints, and non-profit is the best way to ascertain a sensible, dispassionate and truthful outlook.

Bad news spreads faster than good, and when the statement has no context such as the 140-character tweets on Twitter, it's a problem because it's neither defendable nor possible to make sense of something so inflammatory.

Bonding and atonement

Atonement means "at-one-ment" which is the intimate connection between people for example in a jazz band, or soldiers fighting in the war, or the means to physically and mentally feel physically and mentally great.

Bonding together is an essential part of civilised society and religion, the key is who is welcome or unwelcome to these groups. Christian faith should welcome everyone with grace.

Grace is the ability to put the past behind, forgive and move forwards without holding a grudge. Grace acknowledges the human plight, so is critical to maintain wellbeing and reduce anger.

It is when we feel loved and valued for who we are that we perform at our best

The conditions for peace must be law-abiding and a shared simple top-level ideal, such as "love God and other people." And then we need to ACT on it.

In this group, like Wikipedia contributors, people have a chance of exploring the truth through open truthful speech.

The alternative is imitating a lower level unengaging ideal, and if it's secular, not personified, we CANNOT imitate it, so it's useless.

So, the business hierarchy is

- **Truth**
- Social factors
- Faith ethical factors

Untruthfulness is probably becoming attractive to people when businesses become or are meaningless, because people can find something in some emotive mantras: certainty and rally behind, regardless of whether it is right or wrong.

Paraphrasing Jordan Peterson,

"Almost all of our ideas are wrong, and unchallenged ideas become our truths."

So productive, open, challenging dialogue is critical to stay on track.

Handling Flawed arguments

The neo-Marxist mantra with power being the overarching corrupting force in society is worth arguing with because of its lazy thinking and label. But it's worth noting that it's a generalisation and negative generals are all flawed. So, if the debate ensues on the basis that it's a useful starting point it will go nowhere because it's a generalisation without context so will lead to conflict. So ask, "can you give me some specific examples?". Then a sensible discussion can take place as a means to avoid conflict of general vs generalisation.

So, what are the options – tech utopia?

Utopias such as defi are dangerous because they require strict conformity. The c19 violent history of Marxism shows the need for conformity and suggests this conformity leads to violence. Silencing disparate views leaves no other option other than violence to communicate.

decentralized systems. But they will only exist inside the legacy system, and the centralists will have to jump on board. If you think China's social credit system can't come to the western world, where they digitally punish bad behavior such as jaywalking by deducting your "privileges", look at some of the latest policies that western world politicians have proposed. Vaccine passports are highly discriminative, pushing the most marginalized into a tougher position, yet many support it.

This will only fuel the fire more. Everything the elites do to try to stop decentralist outflows will make it worse. What happens when half the population feels their freedoms are under threat? What happens when half the population reaches breaking point? Something has to give. This is civil unrest waiting to happen, but it does not have to end in a civil war. The way out remains simple: the elites must admit their system has failed and come clean. The size and complexity of government have to shrink otherwise the decentralists will flee, otherwise we'll witness the segregation of society manifest as decentralist private cities and centralist legacy cities, a hunger games-esque reality, a Matrix-esque world where the elites are the robots, enabling the decentralists to live within Zion's walls.

The rise of private cities and the resulting bifurcation of society is not a certainty but if the financially repressive status quo of rock-bottom interest rates, rampant inflation, and out-of-control money printing continues, it's unavoidable. In an interview between Marco Wützer — who's somewhat of a

medium.com/concoda/cryptocurrencies-are-about-to-tear-our-society-apart-e0325415be4f

So, in a defi society who is in control, or who do you want to be in control, techies or a democracy?

Michael Jackson • 2nd
Venture Capitalist
13h • 🌐

+ Follow

Have heard loads of complaints about Softbank's London team. Softbank has hired a lot of douchebags from Deutsche Bank. Unsurprisingly Softbank has a douchebag culture full of douchebag behavior. Always avoid DBs from ...see more

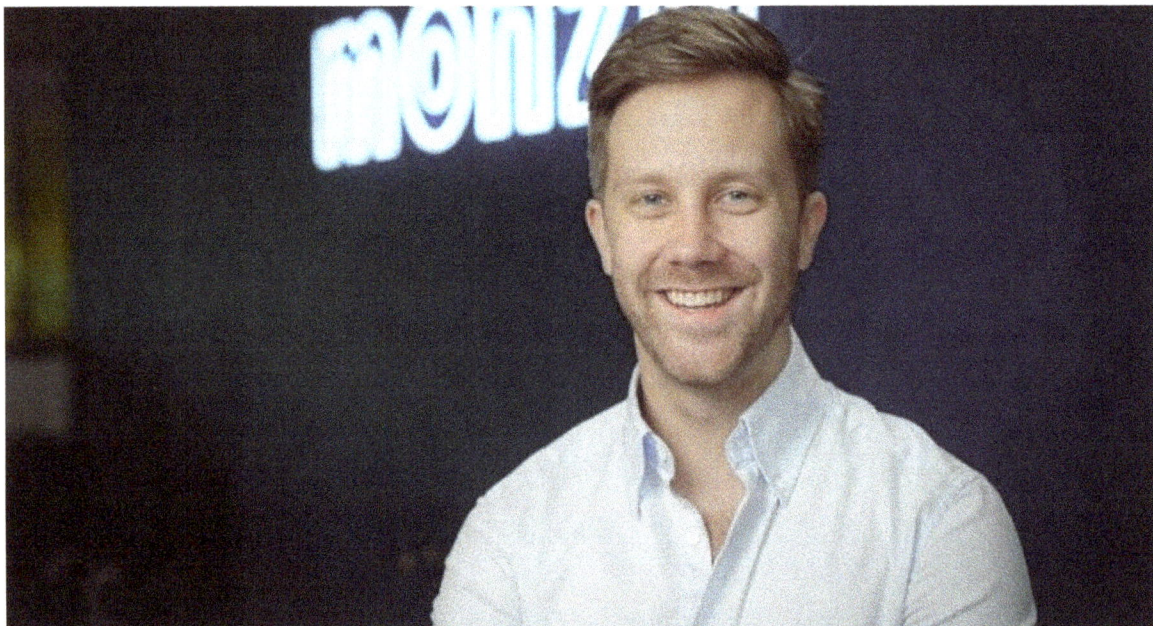

SoftBank partner took investor meeting barefoot and smoking, says Monzo founder

sifted.eu • 3 min read

When you put it all in plain English, everything you can do with cryptocurrency is exactly what you can do with any other form of money. The only big difference I see is that it can now happen outside the domain and authority of governments.

In short, a technocracy.

I don't know if I want keyboard jocks in control of my money, any more than I want Janet Yellen or Jerome Powell. At least with my green paper money, I know I won't wake up to find out it dropped 20 percent overnight because a billionaire was in a bad mood.

medium.datadriveninvestor.com/maybe-you-shouldve-listened-to-that-clueless-girl-about-bitcoin-(

Bitcoin will never go green.

With hindsight, the most intriguing question is why these companies were given such a free ride for so long. One major reason is that the areas in which they most aggressively innovated were lawless, in the sense that at the time there was no applicable law that might have hindered them. So their prevailing mindset that "it's easier to ask forgiveness than to seek permission" was allowed to run amok. Another is that governments were so dazzled by the technology — and so paralysed by neoliberal notions of the alleged inadequacy of the state — that they just let the creative destruction rip. But the biggest problem of all was that we collectively took tech companies at their own valuation. The people who founded these outfits all maintained that they were not like the evil capitalists of old. They were cool, young, idealistic, smart and never, ever wore suits. They supported the Democrats and had mantras such as "don't be evil" in their filings to regulators. What we omitted to notice was that the companies they founded were just corporations. And once they went public they did what corporations do: maximise shareholder value, come what may, avoid regulation and pay as little tax as possible. Just like tobacco companies and arms manufacturers, in fact. It has taken a long time for these pennies to drop, but better late than never.

Top highlight

medium.com/the-guardian/how-silicon-valleys-whiz-kids-finally-ran-out-of-friends-f80fc08edad3

Crypto facilitated by the blockchain structure is a subset and the building blocks of a tech utopia. The mass psychosis of the echo chambers, are fuelled by underlying mantras with a notion such as that "corrupt governments have been deflating your currency and wealth for years."

Yet there are, at times of recession, when printing money makes sense to keep the economy from collapsing and causing a far larger crisis and or mitigating unnecessary damage done by a downturn, that with funding, time will resolve. Yet whilst the question is ambiguous, 92% of the respondents to this survey wanted a decentralised solution.

Fredrik Johansson • 1st
Founder at Libonomy
1w • 🌐

What do you want for your future, be your own bank or let others control your assets.

Decentralized or Centralised?
The author can see how you vote. Learn more

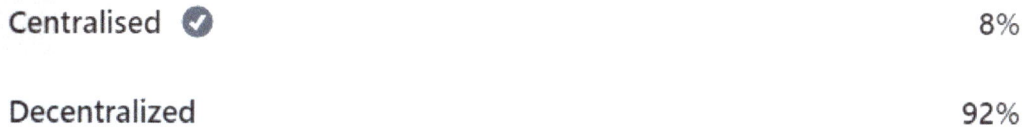

Centralised ✓   8%

Decentralized   92%

168 votes • Poll closed • Remove vote

👍 13 • 5 comments

Reactions

+5

Historically, governments have, at national level, controlled currency and distribution of wealth via taxation, and interest rates, and to a degree managed debt and currency valuation via inflation. In democracies, this has been and should be targeted with the broader interests of the population and the vulnerable in society in mind. Democracy allows for the fact that if the Government messes up, they get voted out.

The notion of defi self-governance, and that you will remain in control in a decentralised finance defi-centric society, is nonsense because there will have to be governance anyway.

With a centralised defi society the governance structure is far more tyrannical with atomised "with control" at the individual level. In order to ascertain voting rights on the myriad of subjects governments look after in a defi society, people will have to be measured upon some sort of social scoring system defining who will be allowed or qualified to vote or not.

Is SEC becoming a joke?

"SEC Chairman Gary Gensler said at an Aspen Institute appearance this ...see more

It's Time To End The SEC's 'Clarity' Charade On Crypto

forbes.com • 5 min read

Something like this lies ahead for the titans of Silicon Valley. The forces driving public disillusionment with their companies are many and varied. They include the sociopathic failure of some of the founders of these outfits to appreciate the consequences of their deployment of digital technology. Exhibit A in this regard is the Facebook boss, Mark Zuckerberg, but there are many other of his ilk among his peers in Silicon Valley. Then there's the fact that the future that tech giants aspire to bring about no longer looks so attractive to ordinary citizens, who see their communities, jobs, societies and politics being screwed by tech giants.

The companies themselves are engines of inequality, enriching tiny elites while laying waste to whole swaths of our economies. The unscrupulous ethos of the surveillance capitalism that some of them practise now looks as distasteful as the financial capitalism that brought about the banking catastrophe of 2008. And we are beginning to realise that the immense power that the valley's uber-geeks have acquired is what Stanley Baldwin memorably nailed as "power without responsibility — the prerogative of the harlot throughout the ages".

medium.com/the-guardian/how-silicon-valleys-whiz-kids-finally-ran-out-of-friends-f80fc08edad3

Cyber Risks

Time for business critical thinking and time to de-digitise / reduce reliance on digital - Increasing digitisation increases exposure to the undefendable cyber risks - China control AI and quantum and we have no chance of defending against Chinas cyber threats, Russia are just playing at it.

China will choose the worst time execute their cyber threat as they always do.

Cyberwar, Part Two: "Flipping Switches"

gatestoneinstitute.org • 1 min read

This tyrannical misalignment of actions and beliefs is the cause of stress in people, and once normalised in a corporate or culture causes mental illness and psychosis.

Attacks on identity

The Irish Post EST·1970 Celebrating 50 years   NEWS ˅   CULTURE ˅   LIFE & STYLE ˅   ENTERT

TRENDING: COVID-19   ALEC BALDWIN   AER LINGUS   MURDER   FACE MASKS   COVID-19 VACCINE   IRISH PUB   T

MANCHESTER University has told students not to use the word 'mother' in an attempt to promote inclusive and diversity.

As part of its newly released 'Guide to inclusive language', formed by the University's so-called 'equality, diversity and inclusion team', the word 'mother' and indeed 'father' have been blacklisted, branded insensitive and not safe for use on campus.

Students are being told to use the word 'parent' or 'guardian' instead.

A reminder that it's Parent or Guardian's Day this Sunday, so don't forget to send your Parent or Guardian some flowers, and be sure to give her - oh, I'm sorry - 'them' a call.

That's right, words like 'her/him' and 'he/she' are off the cards too, as are the following terms and phrases:

Tech-fuelled fragility and the loss of identity caused by identity politics propaganda undermines the basic facts of life:

- the beauty of the male and female role in society
- mothers and fathers

Identity politics is ultimately not about diversity. The outcome of challenging the basics of your identity means a complete loss of your purpose and leaves you nothing to fight for. This leaves people with integrity who care and run into the cancel culture, vulnerable to suicide. People who lose themselves become fragile, how will our Gen Z kids ever know themselves?

"The privilege of a lifetime is to become who you truly are." Carl Jung

The drip-drip effect

This menticide has crept upon us. Waves of terror and isolation have made us aware of the importance of relationships, but notice how the same woke and tech tyrannies still prevail in the residual silence?

This leaves so many CEOs with their actions and beliefs misaligned unaware that their flawed panicky tech strategies and loss of meaning are costing their people a mental health crisis.

Investment in technology for the first time in 40 years has become the biggest investment category having just overtaken oil. So, it's no mean challenge and has a massive PR / menticide machine behind it!

Accountability

Who is accountable for defi? Can you vote against the defi decentralised option? If crypto crashed right now there is NO recourse for "investors."

The cost of speaking out against these technology-fuelled mass psychoses is alienation. This alienation is without recourse to the law or accountability, and in fact, usurps the law. The impact is that your phone stops ringing, you may be labelled as being toxic, ostracised, and your online past "informally investigated", thereby usurping the law.

Lily Hajdu-Gimes, a Hungarian psychoanalyst, diagnosed the trauma of forced conformity in patients, as well as in herself. "I play the game that is offered by the regime," she told friends. "Though as soon as you accept that rule you are in a trap."

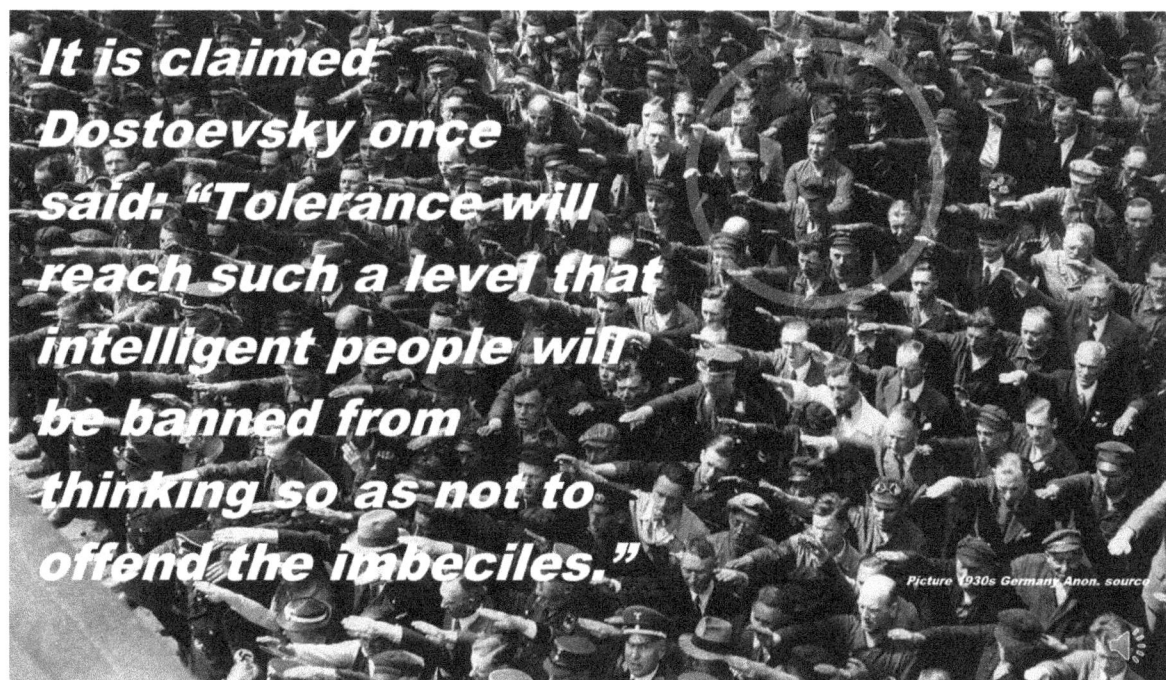

It is claimed Dostoevsky once said: "Tolerance will reach such a level that intelligent people will be banned from thinking so as not to offend the imbeciles."

Picture 1930s Germany. Anon. source

What's the leadership / societal challenge?

We are our worst enemies, and our greatest threat is when mental illness becomes the norm, or a psychic epidemic or mass psychosis takes hold.

The rise of the victim leads to tyranny and menticide and a hopelessly vulnerable state.

Consider "are you in a hopelessly vulnerable state or too vulnerable or fearful to challenge the woke mantras?"

Mass hysteria or mass psychosis

Mass hysteria or mass psychosis is an extreme form of groupthink when members of the group follow the consensus instead of thinking critically and valuing the truth and healthy open debate to inform decisions.

George Orwell said, *"in a time of universal deceit, telling the truth is a revolutionary act!"*

"What is needed now is a swift cold shower of reality. The time for self-harming distractions with "wokus pocus," obsessing about sexual dysmorphia, Marxist "critical race theory" and "climate catastrophism" ... - all of which the Chinese Communist Party is glad to encourage - must end." Gatestone Institute 19/8/21

What are you too afraid to discuss that you know needs to be challenged and thought through?

How do false truths and ideology gain traction?

Illusion or ideology gather support during tough times of non-reality because ideology affords people the luxury to deny, blame and distance themselves from reality. Victimhood is a convenient position. The falsehood is convenient and provides a means of creating certainty and unity with others, and a radical spirit, drive, and purpose.

Falsehoods often dominate ideology and gather traction because they normalise and provide flawed: purpose; group identity; and a weird sense of moral high ground.

People can't cope with uncertainty so no matter how weird the ideology, it creates a sense of certainty and moral virtuousness and righteousness, even when the bases of the ideology are patently false.

The falsehood creates a blindspot, which closes the counterargument.

Certainty is particularly attractive when all else is falling apart. However, the flawed ideology typified, highlighted by the predominant mantra or generalisation, is always at the root cause of a crisis.

This is psychologically the cause of a company turnaround, where the generalisation creates a blind spot. This distortion or deletion causes strategy to miss the real issues, by distorting or deleting the facts. Most "company turnaround practitioners" and business leaders completely miss this mechanism so get duped by the comfortable mantras and lazy thinking that beautifully justifies the status quo.

People will always do all they can to do what they want to do and be left alone.

The misleading language

The postmodern words and mantras used are centred around emotionally charged subjects such as race, sexuality, or minorities. This is where people can choose to feel marginalised or hard done by or victimised. This victimhood leads to scapegoating around very divisive clever general mantras, lacking specifics and context. This divides groups.

The dire Woke narrative around victimhood.

Victimhood is the most unhealthy psychology yet for many tragically attractive... **Your lived experience will materialize unless you take responsibility and action.**

What is stopping anyone?

Woke language is clever at fuelling division, a moral high ground, and exclusivity such as Black Lives Matter. The next level of distortion critical race theory when looking at everything through a racial lens, with white people being the perpetrators so unable to comment, is patently nonsense un-true, as well as rightly angering good well-meaning white people with the appalling false accusation of implicitly being racist.

Specifically, do you see how the headings "Black Lives Matter" and "critical race theory" or "post-modernism" create division and distortion?

Penalties

The penalties that maintain the tyranny and silence debate

The scapegoats that infringe the ideology get an aggressive, emotive, personal protective dialogue and with vicious slurs and labels. These vicious labels are designed to scare off challengers.

Specifically: how do you respond to these vicious flawed labels when you challenge these mantras? What EQ skills do you need to do that and what is the awareness to develop our skills?

Yet our hubris shows we are unaware of the need to develop our strategies:

07:23		15:46
← ⋮		← ⋮

Peter Brown · 2nd
Director B2B North…
1w · 🌐
+ Follow

Do you have what it takes to succeed ?
The author can see how you vote. **Learn more**

YES ✓	87%
NO	10%
OTHER, answer in comments	2%

1,336 votes • Poll closed • **Remove vote**

😊😯❤️ 200 · · · · 149 comments

Like · Comment · Share · Send

Reactions

Comments · · · Most relevant

Leave your thoughts here… · @ · Post

Tom Pickering FIET
CEO, Special Situations Director…
2w · 🌐

At work, do you feel increasingly:
You can see how people vote. **Learn more**

isolated and lonely	0%
valued and included	9%
collaborative with peers?	27%
working self sufficiently? ✓	64%

11 votes • Poll closed • **Remove vote**

👍 2 · · · 1 comment • 750 views

Like · Comment · Share · Send

📈 **750 views of your post**

Reactions

Leave your thoughts here… · @ · Post

Do you see how the underlying thinking in the dialogue and these terms are used to attack and create exclusive echo chambers and attack conflicting views from the moral high ground such as Christianity or any other faith?

How do you challenge the ideology?

Our natural inclination is to reject ideas that don't fit our taste and defy error that damages our illusion, mantra, or ideology.

These mantras can be seemingly positive such as rejecting views that don't fit with your version of the truth. This creates blind spots.

Whoever challenges woke illusions conveniently becomes a victim of scapegoating, and so will be met with anger. Anger because you are challenging the fundamental woke or another anchor, which could be that person's means of "coping or finding meaning, woke group religion, and or of course the pain of denying they could be wrong."

Specifically: Do you see truth as a journey and take an interest in finding out the merits of other people's conflicting views, before taking your view?

Why is a challenge to ideology met with anger? In their heart of hearts, they know what they are doing is wrong so can't sufficiently articulate a response to the challenge, so anger is a convenient and last form of defence.

The ideology traps

The ideology trap is when we lose touch with reality and live in a delusional state. So we habitually look for information that fits with our delusion and therefore reject anything else, ***without thinking,*** leaving us vulnerable to:

- social media echo chambers
- negative emotions
- panic
- isolation
- fear

Conforming actions creates waves of fear so maintains tyranny
You might not see how using "pronouns" could fuel evil.
I added pronouns to my header because "I could not see a downside", or I'm "not sure why I should *not* use pronouns."
Acting by adding pronouns forces us to realign our beliefs and get drawn in. This is akin to saluting

Hitler or what is underlying the ideology. This draws us in, and flawed actions trap us.

It starts with something baseless and flawed and part of woke ideology such as the pronoun aspect of identity politics. The iterative tools of tyranny are:

- to create waves of fear
- nonsensical waves of propaganda that make no sense
- digitally deselecting information

There is a link between adding pronouns and or saluting Hitler. Both are wrong and falling victim to tyranny, whilst the methods were different, the victim, scapegoating and terror/silencing processes are the same.

"He/Him""She/Her"

These gender pronouns corrupt through the trauma of forced conformity in patients:

"I play the game that is offered by the regime," she told friends, "though as soon as you accept that rule you are in a trap."

Lily Hajdu-Gimes

The woke terror now is found on social media, in the form of marginalisation, public attacks, and labelling. Marginalisation on social media creates the equivalent emotional and physiological response akin to being physically attacked.

Menticide

Tech ideology and mantras such as "tech is the future", "digital disruption", "governments can't be trusted" have led to the panic and corruption of tech investing, which are often drifting no more than to become a Ponzi scheme.

Most of these Techcos lack meaning let alone a compelling proposition, yet the product, system, social media, and information are subject to manipulation using diversionary general self-fulfilling language, such as "decentralised finance" or "*social* media"!

The perceived valuations of these often loss-making tech entities are driven by burning cash to inflate valuations, and a focus on growth, and domination.

During this process, professionals and leaders get duped so become compromised, so morality becomes compromised, and greed takes hold.

Many are unaware of the tech menticide or collective madness that is occurring, leading to confusion, and panic. But it is hard to admit and reverse.

Trapped in the present

People are trapped in the present because of their addiction to social media. They are unable to step out of the endless propaganda leading to some weird outcomes and waves of untruths:

- postmodernism defines science as a man-made construct
- men can get pregnant
- gender pronouns
- lived experience
- taking offence
- critical race theory
- tech is the future
- victimhood is in control
- labelling: racist, sexist, transphobic

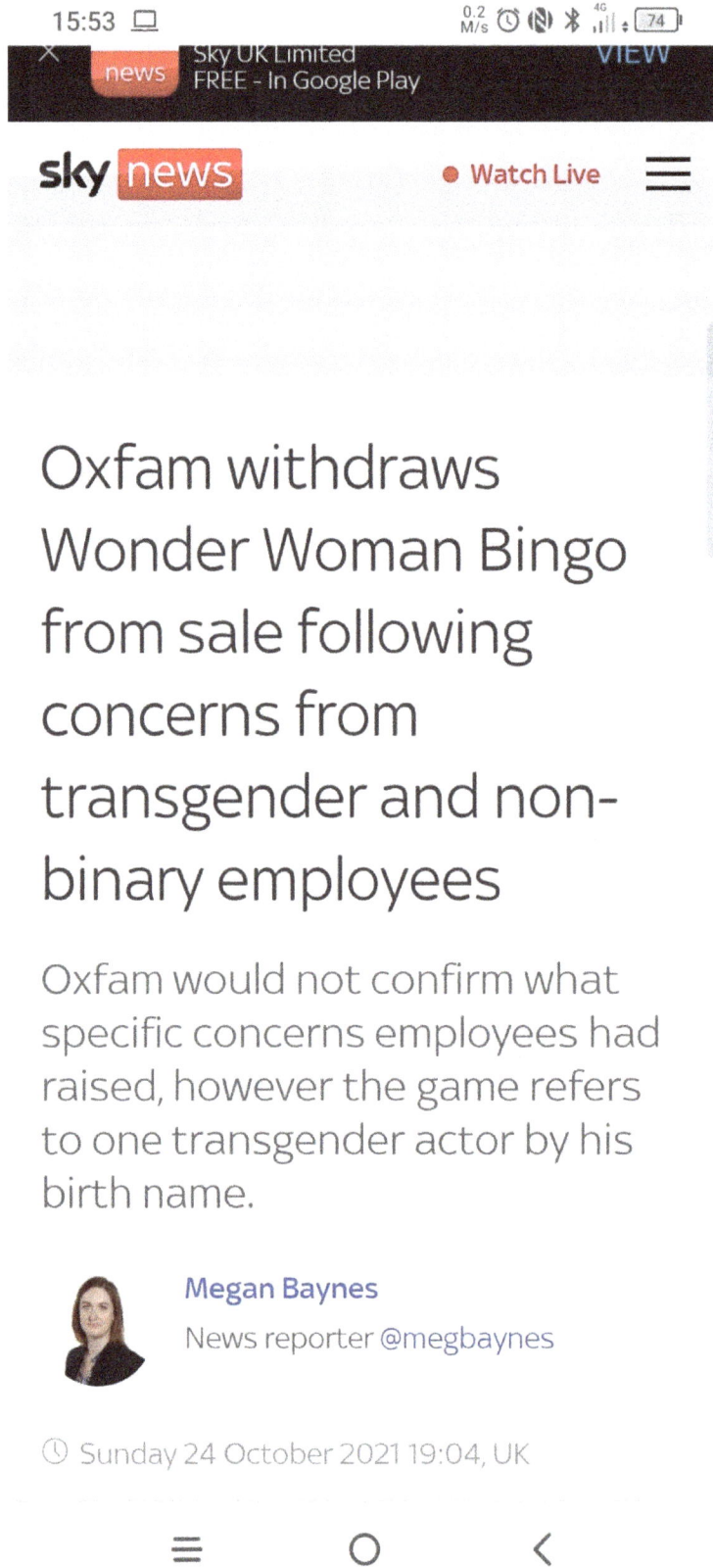

15:53

Sky UK Limited
FREE - In Google Play

VIEW

sky news

● Watch Live

Oxfam withdraws Wonder Woman Bingo from sale following concerns from transgender and non-binary employees

Oxfam would not confirm what specific concerns employees had raised, however the game refers to one transgender actor by his birth name.

Megan Baynes
News reporter @megbaynes

Sunday 24 October 2021 19:04, UK

Unicoms pregnant man emoji

Propaganda weakens people and their resolve

Propaganda creates psychosis because it's delusional. It weakens people and makes people vulnerable to a saviour such as Xi or Jesus.

"It is not for nothing that our age calls for the redeemer personality, for the one who can emancipate himself from the inescapable grip of the collective and save at least his own soul, who lights a beacon of hope for others, proclaiming that there is at least one man who has succeeded in extricating himself from that fatal identity with the group psyche. For the group, because of its unconsciousness, has no freedom of choice, and so psychic activity runs on in it like an uncontrolled law of nature. There is thus set going a chain reaction that comes to a stop only in catastrophe." Carl Jung

This propaganda-fuelled psychosis eventually creates menticide which is when totalitarianism takes hold. Currently, menticide is manifesting in many forms.

- woke ideology: postmodernism
- China Communist party ideals
- Defi utopia, Bigtech ideology, cryptocurrency

Totalitarianism is the greatest threat people face. It is based on a flawed assumption that the ruler is themselves, another human, and NOT God. This does not fit with the flawed nature of people, people are flawed and know so little and are therefore completely incapable of fulfilling this role.

Total power

Total power corrupts, and the masses become childlike, transforming sound minds to sick minds. As a check, "what is the alternative view to this propaganda"?:

- the use of pronouns
- gender usurps biological sex
- "tech is the future"
- crypto: "FIAT currencies and government institutions are corrupt"

The last point is one of a culture turning upon itself, causing good-thinking, well-intentioned people to turn on and blame their governments and institutions, rather than take personal responsibility. The issue is the same: victimhood. Blame and propaganda signify and maintain victimhood.

Ideology creates a childlike state

Totalitarianism leads to mass suffering and social ruin. Ideology, rather than free thought, dominates and becomes accepted, killing the mind or menticide.

This self-righteousness with a set of attack tools is a comfortable place for people or groups who feel victimised, proving the opportunity to cling on to flawed ideals, such as wokeness. From there, there is high ground and battles to fight from which they attack others, rather than take responsibility for searching out the facts.

This is a childlike state operating in tyrannical ideals. Self-righteousness is found by attacking those that don't fit with these ideals.

Disgust and waves of terror and the stupid mind

Hitler often used words of disgust when referring to the Jews. Disgust makes it easy to isolate responsibility and obsessively scapegoat and wipe out your targets. Manmade, moral matrixes like these are dangerous and nonfactual territory that create conflict that's nearly impossible to rationalise.

It is more comfortable to believe ideals than to face the facts. Facing the facts requires skill, intelligence, courage, and competence to action.

Waves of terror interspersed with periods of calm, cause morals to sink and soften people up to become manipulatable and non-thinking.

Propaganda is comfortable because it provides meaning and normalises this madness, and creates a weird sort of meaning and purpose causing once good people to become revolutionaries for the ideology.

Like postmodernism, that believes truth is a man-made construct, and the second wave lie "lived experience usurps the truth."

Lived experience is tough to challenge because it's illogical. Although a half-truth without context is so more appealing than reason. It gives the cowardly, stupid, and less able mind real power, gained through a self-righteous ideology and a set of tools, and ready-made team of supporters to attack and cancel those who dare to challenge what doesn't fit their ideology or can see through the woke lies.

Turning on your own and isolation

The addictive nature of social media and fear of attack causes people to become vulnerable to propaganda and turn on their own. This is how to obfuscate and hide the truth. For example, CCP members are openly attacking America for their errors now on LinkedIn, under a higher moral guise Xi! The ultimate totalitarian. LinkedIn is the only social media approved by China.

"Indeed, it is becoming ever more obvious," he writes, *"that it is not famine, not earthquakes, not microbes, not cancer but the man himself who is man's greatest danger to man, for the simple reason that there is no adequate protection against psychic epidemics, which are infinitely more devastating than the worst of natural catastrophes."* Carl Jung, *The Symbolic Life.*

". . .the totalitarian systems of the 20th century represent a kind of collective psychosis. Whether gradually or suddenly, reason and common human decency are no longer possible in such a system: there is only a pervasive atmosphere of terror, and a projection of "the enemy," imagined to be "in our midst." Thus society turns on itself, urged on by the ruling authorities." Joost Merloo *The Rape of the Mind.*

When we can't cope, we will normalise things to make sense, justify inaction, and cope in a vain attempt to justify the status quo.

Very few saw the rise of Hitler as being a problem, yet a few did.

Taming the strong

Language is deceptive and changing it is powerful: rather than connecting us, social media isolates us. Isolation is the perfect tool to disrupt the healthy dialogue interactions that keep us in check. These healthy interactions enable us to see through propaganda. Isolation, however, enables new patterns of thought to be formed and tames wild animals.

Isolation in combination with waves of terror or uncertainty, cause many people to reach a hopelessly vulnerable state. In this state we crave certainty, which can be any form of certainty, many will make bad decisions to reach a point of certainty.

Turning on institutions

Action is very visible and always imperfect, so tough times challenge morality and social norms. This causes good people to attack the institutions that keep them safe. So ideologies like "FIAT currencies have robbed the masses" or claims that "governments are corrupt" justify cryptocurrency and create blind spots preventing with no thought as to the costs, broader social, or moral considerations.

This ideology is convenient for investors who are panicked by having nothing good to invest in, by pumping up the valuations of cryptocurrency. Non-compelling untrusted fintech models are ideal.

These tech businesses largely give away their services with losses fuelled by ever-increasing equity investment rounds that bump up valuations. These are very like a Ponzi scheme version with each investment round passing the parcel. These valuations are based upon and fuelled by the internal sub ideologies of these tech businesses, creating their own unchallenged echo systems and convenient terms "bitboys" or "nocoiners" to describe their respective echo chambers to fuel their ideology and isolate others.

So, given the priority is to stabilise the economy post-pandemic, cryptocurrency is the antithesis of a solution, ill-thought-out, raising more questions about its fundamental implications that require a fundamental review versus the unspecified gains through streamlining bank processes using blockchain.

- Liquidity is a big issue with crypto in relation to drawing cash away from fractional reserve banking mechanisms in the retail banking sector.
- The ever-increasing power consumption of bitcoin alone increases and is currently 50% of the UK's power consumption. Ever-increasing because this is related to the increasing escalating and unstoppable cyber-security concern risks from China?
- There is an onslaught of lies and assumptions about crypto such as "stable coins" will be underpinned by assets, drawing away further liquidity from the productive economy?
- Crypto "stable coins" are surely another misleading mantra and a contradiction in terms?
- Volatile valuations will drag investment away from FIAT currencies undermining solvency - the complete opposite of the mitigating bank balance sheets post 2008.
- The increased reliance on digital will leave the UK wide open to cyber-attacks from China.

- Paraphrasing the chair of the UK APPG on Ai discussing crypto adoption said last night (27 Oct 2021), he quelled a discussion following a few tough questions from doubters raising issues re crypto viability "well it's happening".

INNOVATION

China's New Quantum Computer Has 1 Million Times the Power of Google's

And they say it's the world's fastest.

By Brad Bergan
Oct 27, 2021

An abstract depiction of a data channel.   spainter_vfx / iStock

It appears a quantum computer rivalry is growing between the U.S. and China.

Physicists in China claim they've constructed two quantum computers with performance speeds that outrival competitors in the U.S., debuting a superconducting machine, in addition to an even speedier one that uses light photons to obtain unprecedented results, according to a recent study published in the peer-reviewed journals *Physical Review Letters* and *Science Bulletin*.

China has exaggerated the capabilities of its technology before, but such soft spins are usually tagged to defense tech, which means this new feat could be the real deal.

China's quantum computers still make a lot of errors

"he who dictates and formulates the words and phrases we use, he who is master of the press and radio, is master of the mind." —— Joost A.M. Meerloo, *The Rape of the Mind: The Psychology of Thought Control, Menticide, and Brainwashing.*

"Where thinking is isolated without free exchange with other minds and can no longer expand, delusion may follow. Whenever ideas are compartmentalized, behind and between curtains, the process of continual alert confrontation of facts and reality is hampered. The system freezes, becomes rigid, and dies of delusion." —— Joost A.M. Meerloo, *The Rape of the Mind: The Psychology of Thought Control, Menticide, and Brainwashing.*

"There is another important weapon the totalitarians use in their campaign to frighten the world into submission. This is the weapon of psychological shock. Hitler kept his enemies in a state of constant confusion and diplomatic upheaval. They never knew what this unpredictable madman was going to do next. Hitler was never logical because he knew that that was what he was expected to be. Logic can be met with logic, while illogic cannot—it confuses those who think straight. The Big Lie and monotonously repeated nonsense have more emotional appeal in a cold war than logic and reason. While the enemy is still searching for a reasonable counter-argument to the first lie, the totalitarians can assault him with another." —— Joost A.M. Meerloo, *The Rape of the Mind: The Psychology of Thought Control, Menticide, and Brainwashing*

Ideology provides certainty

Tech, Woke, and China versions of totalitarianism tragically provide this certainty when people are at their wit's end. Divisive language creates a revolutionary zeal caused by a good society to turn on itself when things are too easy. This strategy is far easier than taking personal responsibility.

It's far easier and more comfortable to be a victim than to face your failings and find the courage to consider and face the future and plan accordingly.

Jesus said, "The proud are an abomination" and for this very reason they have no chance of turning to their saviour.

"I am the way, the truth, and the life. No one comes to the Father except through me" Jesus said in John 14:6.

The scale of the challenge is daunting because at its most basic level it's a battle between:

1. Growth and domination – the current insatiable madness
2. Profit and relationships – back – basics - realigned mantras

Bitcoin and Silicon Valley have a whole anti-establishment aspect to it, and this creates an odd link with symptoms of the CCP tyranny that are trying to undermine Western values and institutions.

However, the secular outcome is a pathological order with no spontaneity, curiosity, no beauty or joy.

So, what could prevent this menticide?

Create a parallel structure to:

- reset relationships
- rationalise businesses viability and valuation based upon profit
- enable the right people with integrity to thrive
- face the truth – tools to identify and understand the distortions
- challenge ideology to check truth and validity
- open dialogue and identify the blind spots
- create personal responsibility
- create empathy to acknowledge others
- value different views
- take lots of self-realised actions
- provide grace, forgiveness, and love

You gotta understand that **some people never really grow.**

They never learn their lesson.
They never recognize their mistakes, they never acknowledge their faults, they never admit they were in the wrong. You will never receive an apology from them, and you will never see their behavior change.

Bakwaaas

Wimps and cowards thrive in a woke culture because they don't have to face reality or take responsibility for their actions so can only focus on avoiding debate, attacking, and destroying.

The misleading language

Woke language is clever at fuelling division, by creating a moral high ground and exclusivity victimhood such as Black Lives Matter. The next level of distortion is critical race theory, which looks at everything through a racial lens, with white people being the perpetrators unable to comment. This patently untrue nonsense also angers good, well-meaning white people with the appalling false accusation of implicitly being white and therefore being a racist!

Specifically, do you see how the headings "Black Lives Matter" and "critical race theory" or "postmodernism" create division and distortion?

Handling Flawed arguments

The neo-Marxist mantra that power is the overarching corrupting force in society is worth arguing with because it's lazy thinking. But it's a generalisation, and negative generals are all flawed. So, if the debate ensues on the basis that the pretext is a useful starting point, it will go nowhere because it's a generalisation without context, which will lead to conflict.

"Abuse of Power?" The solution is to ask "can you give me some specific examples?" Only then can a sensible discussion take place as a rational means to avoid conflict of generalisation vs generalisation.

How do you challenge the ideology?

Our natural inclination is to reject ideas or perceived threats that don't fit our taste and defy error that damages our illusion, mantra, or ideology.

These mantras can be seemingly positive such as we are the "Best in Class." They create blind spots.

Whoever challenges woke illusions conveniently becomes a victim of scapegoating, so will be met with anger. Anger because you are challenging the fundamental anchor, which could be that person's means of "coping or finding meaning, or the pain of denying they could be wrong."

Specifically: Do you see truth as a journey and take an interest in finding out the merits of other people's conflicting views before taking your view?

Why is a challenge to ideology met with anger? In their hearts of hearts, they know what they are doing is wrong but can't sufficiently articulate a response to the challenge. So anger is a convenient and last form of defence.

Breaking the cycle and realising infinite capability

By taking lots of small actions you break the tyrannical cycle. This enables people to realise the value of their peers and the value of themselves to their peers, so, the outcome is self-fulfilling.

For example, by putting others first you create a self-virtuous cycle but only if self-actioned rather than purely taught. Experiential learning is enabled by taking new action from a different perspective. This is the way we learn. See, you have the infinite capability. The infinite element is through a connection with God or else your limit is you!

The best place to be is somewhere like realising that we are all flawed, and no human has the ability to act as God and set the rules, judge morality and or set the way anyone thinks.

Businesses in turnaround scenarios descend into tyranny and exhibit the same traits, and the appropriate response is not more tyranny. Rather, people need love, oneness, reconnection, and clarity. not more dictum to resolve what has become unconsciously for them, their self-made psychology, that has created their own impossible scenarios.

Correctly facilitated with the correct perspectives this new self-realised action immediately gets results, because immediate new actions are taken, courage is overcome and so perspectives permanently shifted.

It's a difficult process, but once the ball starts rolling it's exciting like a new flower coming out or a jazz band that can fluently play a completely new set of improvised tunes. TOGETHER.

Winningthinking.uk®

By using winningthinking®, we have got businesses back to profit and cash in 2 weeks and cash weeks from haemorrhaging £400k/month. So new action works immediately, and the new shifts create immediate results, cash, profits, and refreshed relationships, and reset mental health. It fixes the right problem that drives everything: the perspectives and the thinking.

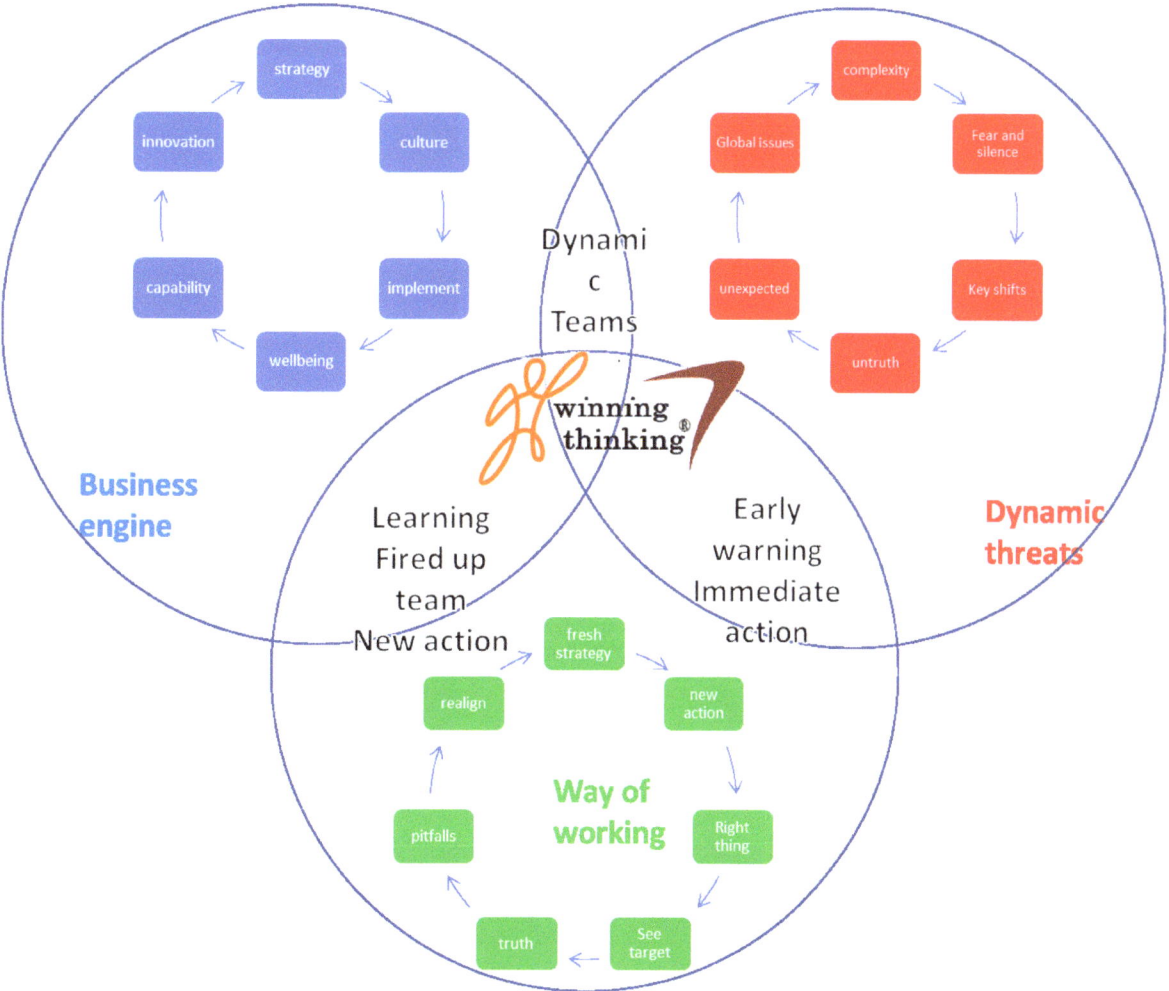

This realignment restores and creates new energy.

The misalignment

But look at the action CEOs are taking, fuelled by the Big 4, leading to more panicky fractious investment in technology. Technology is the antithesis and fuels menticide and mental ill-health.

Mai-Britt Poulsen • 1st
Managing Director and Senior Partner, Head of BCG for UK, Netherlands and...
2d • Edited • 🌐

We are just a week away from #COP26 and #sustainability is on everyone's mind. Or as my colleague, Norbert Faure puts it: "sustainability is a global agenda". In this episode of #WithMaiBritt, I discuss with him the role of technology in the climate journey and ask the one very crucial question – "Are the tech leaders aware of the difference they can make?".

Norbert's Team has already proved that #technology can provide solutions and scale them on a worldwide level. In our conversation, he shares his experiences from the mining, maritime and financial industries. Watch for more.

#GroupUpForClimate

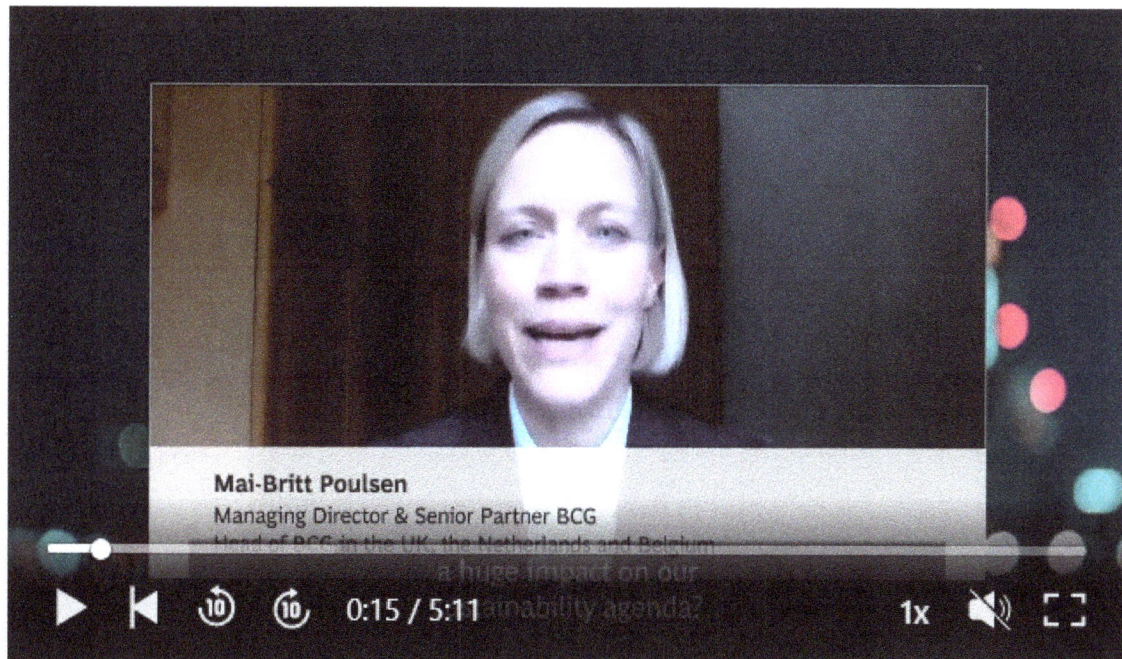

Mai-Britt Poulsen
Managing Director & Senior Partner BCG

▶ ⏮ ↺ ↻ 0:15 / 5:11   1x 🔇 ⛶

👍 🌿 😊 84 • 3 comments • 1.733 views

The risks are high because people are trapped in a tyranny faced with a personal attack for standing against these misnomers. If people are attacked it is tempting for them to apologise and fall in line. This causes people to compromise and lose themselves and their souls or their strength to cope.

"The privilege of a lifetime is to become who you truly are." Carl Jung

Attacks on identity

This tyrannical misalignment of actions and beliefs is the cause of stress in people, and once normalised in a corporate or culture causes mental illness and psychosis.

The Irish Post EST·1970 Celebrating 50 years   NEWS ⌄   CULTURE ⌄   LIFE & STYLE ⌄   ENTERT

TRENDING: COVID-19   ALEC BALDWIN   AER LINGUS   MURDER   FACE MASKS   COVID-19 VACCINE   IRISH PUB   T

MANCHESTER University has told students not to use the word 'mother' in an attempt to promote inclusive and diversity.

As part of its newly released 'Guide to inclusive language', formed by the University's so-called 'equality, diversity and inclusion team', the word 'mother' and indeed 'father' have been blacklisted, branded insensitive and not safe for use on campus.

Students are being told to use the word 'parent' or 'guardian' instead.

A reminder that it's Parent or Guardian's Day this Sunday, so don't forget to send your Parent or Guardian some flowers, and be sure to give her - oh, I'm sorry - 'them' a call.

That's right, words like 'her/him' and 'he/she' are off the cards too, as are the following terms and phrases:

Tech fuelled fragility and the loss of identity caused by identity politics propaganda undermines the basic facts of life:

- the beauty of the male and female role in society
- mothers and fathers

This is ultimately not about diversity the outcome of challenging the basics of identity is a complete loss of purpose and nothing to fight for. This leaves people with integrity facing the cancel culture vulnerable to suicide.

New action

New action from re-aligned paradigms realigns actions get back to humour, new action, freedom, and intimacy.

Winning Thinking
How to Make Strategy & People Engagement Happen

Make People Engagement Happen:

1. Creating a robust purpose
2. Transforming capability
3. Engaging employees
4. Creating commitment
5. Getting everyone thinking
6. Creating Trust

Make Strategy Happen:

1. Achieving breakthrough
2. Creating sustainable profits
3. Freeing Time: are you too busy?
4. Getting everyone implementing
5. Managing risk
6. Staying on track

The drip-drip effect

When to act, it's TOTALLY down to you!?

NOW is the time to take new action. Do you have the skills to face this and realign action?

The Harder the challenge the greater the glory.

It's down to YOU..

August Landmesser was the German that had the nous not to salute at the German rally in Germany in 1936 when a newly built ship was about to leave Hamburg harbour. The photo shows a crowd of people, who are believed to be workers, raising their arms for the infamous saluting gesture, except for a man believed to be August Landmesser who is standing with his arms crossed.

Anonymous source thought to be a rally in a German dockyard in 1935

The bizarre paradox is that whilst the pandemic initially caused us to realise the importance of people to– people relationships during the lockdown, acknowledging and making time for people, this is fading. I expect this inactivity and misalignment could cause the next wave to be more damaging to our well-being..

Critical Thinking

The impact of this menticide is far-reaching, but who is really thinking ahead or planning?

The pandemic has also provided a crisis that we have not addressed its root cause and potential source and blatant cover-up in China.

Take EVs... "When talking about saving the planet by replacing internal combustion vehicles with EVs, we first need to comprehend the scale of this initiative.

Talking strictly about vehicles, we need to face a simple fact, there are an estimated 1 billion cars on the road each year, and this number is increasing.

Considering that most of these vehicles are still using internal combustion engines, replacing all fuel-powered cars with electrics requires a lot of effort.

The most-produced car in the world is the modern Toyota Corolla, with roughly 43 million of them built over the course of 55 years. We do not have 55 years left to stop global warming.

Unless we take action to prevent the sale of used petrol-powered cars to the developing world, our best efforts of replacing traditional transport with the green alternative will soon prove to be in vain. Otherwise, individuals will be tempted to sell their old cars to foreign buyers, as governmental programs may struggle to make a more profitable offer.

While Europe will replace their current vehicles with electric alternatives, the developing economies in Asia and Africa are expected to proceed in the opposite direction.

However, comfort EVs do not come cheap, and the majority of the world cannot afford to buy a brand-new car without special government-funded programs. Not only are such governmental initiatives still rare, but most people would also be required to sell their current vehicle to fund the purchase of a new one.

The question is, what are we going to do with all the used petrol-powered cars?

Even so, car companies still need time to design, develop and market their upcoming electric models, similarly to how the legal infrastructure for the benefits of driving an EV required extended debate.

EVs are not bad. Maybe they are too late.